HIGH COUNTRY HYMNAL

HIGH COUNTRY HYMNAL

Ashlyn McKayla Ohm

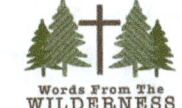

Words from the Wilderness
© 2024 by Ashlyn McKayla Ohm

HIGH COUNTRY HYMNAL

Copyright © 2024 by Ashlyn McKayla Ohm

All rights reserved. Printed in the United States of America. No part of this book may be used or reproduced in any form or by any electronic or mechanical means, including information storage and retrieval systems, without permission in writing from the publisher. The only exception is brief quotations in reviews.

For information, contact
www.wordsfromthewilderness.com

Cover design by Hannah Linder Designs
Formatting template by Derek Murphy

ISBN (paperback): 979-8-9853344-9-4
ISBN (ebook): 979-8-9853344-8-7
Library of Congress Control Number: 2024909290

Unless otherwise noted, Scripture quotations are from The ESV® Bible (The Holy Bible, English Standard Version®), © 2001 by Crossway, a publishing ministry of Good News Publishers. Used by permission. All rights reserved.

First Edition: October 2024
Hot Springs, Arkansas

10 9 8 7 6 5 4 3 2 1
29 28 27 26 25 24

Table of Contents

THE KEY ix

BESIDE THE MEADOW 1
    TESTIMONY 2
    MOUNTAIN YEAR 3
    BLUE MOON 5
    THINNER AIR 6
    MOOSE MUSE 7
    PIKA 9
    WHITE-COLLAR CAGE 11
    THE ROCKIES IN THE FALL 12
    BEAR PAW 15

WITHIN THE FOREST 16
    CAMO 17
    FIRST HIKE 19
    DIFFERENT, THEY CALLED ME 21
    MUSHROOM MIRACLE 23
    MEET YOU IN THE MOUNTAINS 25
    NO MAN'S LAND 26
    THE EDGE OF IT ALL 28
    LOVE AND DEATH AND EVERYTHING ELSE 30
    SHE WHO SENDS US CLIMBING 31
    EAGLE CANYON RAILWAY 32
    ELK CALF 34
    TIMID TRUST 36
    MOOSE CHILD 37
    THE KISSING BRIDGE 38
    BLACK LAKE LOVE 40
    LEVI 41
    LOVE LIKE THE MOUNTAINS 42

ABOVE THE TREELINE 43

TABLE OF CONTENTS

tundra 44
GODFORSAKEN PLACE 46
SANCTUARY 48
THE SHAPE OF GRACE 50
GLACIER GLORY 51
MISSING MOUNTAINS 52
AFTER THE FIRE 54
THINGS TO DO WHEN YOUR WORLD ENDS
(incomplete list) 55
KRUMMHOLZ 56
SNOW 57
DAY AND NIGHT 59
HOW CAN I HELP BUT SING? 61

ALONG THE RIDGE *63*

LEAD ME FORTH 64
MOUNTAIN BROOK 65
EL SHADDAI 67
TRUE NORTH 68
OUZEL 70
SONG OF THE STORM 71
ALPENGLOW 72
TO THE UNTAMED GOD 73
OLYMPUS 76
PROLOGUE 78
ENDING AND BEGINNING 79
TABERNACLE 80
RECLAIMED 81

BEYOND THE HORIZON *83*

INVERSION 84
CANYON ROAD 85
ENTERING HEAVEN 87
LAKE OF DREAMS 89
HEART OF THE MOUNTAINS 91
CONTINENTAL DIVIDE 92

HIGH COUNTRY HYMNAL

- AUTUMN LAKE 94
- ETERNITY 95
- SHEEP LAKES 96
- NEVER SUMMER 98
- STORM PASS 99
- NOVEMBER PRAYER 100
- WALKING WEST 102
- BIRTHDAY CANDLES 103
- HIGH COUNTRY BLESSING 104

THANK YOU! *107*

ACKNOWLEDGMENTS *109*

PHOTO CREDITS *110*

ABOUT THE AUTHOR *111*

KEEP READING! *112*

PRAYERS, PRAISES, PROMISES *113*

THE KEY

I was born with my heart in the shape of a key,
But the lock it was made for was unknown to me.
Still I tried many doors, but not one opened wide
Till I followed my course to the wild mountainside.
And then glorious gates were flung open for me;
I know this is the place where God made me to be.

INTO THE MOUNTAINS...

HIGH COUNTRY HYMNAL

BESIDE THE MEADOW

POEMS OF WARMTH AND WELCOME

HIGH COUNTRY HYMNAL
TESTIMONY

Twenty-one I was, tripping over untested trails,
Still afraid to bleed, and weep, and pray.
It was the gentle hands of grace that stopped my stumble,
Opening a door I had not seen in my wall.
I could say more about it—
The way I wept like a rescued rebel when I saw the land,
The way I ran heart-whole and joy-strong over glacial fields,
The way I shed my shuffling doubts behind the alpenglow, and knew
That my soul was sewn to this place, these peaks, this Presence.
That's the story.
Now my trails have run like rivers through a future
All yet unmapped then—but still
I remember the place where my hope first hovered.
These mountains are steady, and so is my compass.
I return, and return, and return.

BESIDE THE MEADOW
MOUNTAIN YEAR

I love these dear mountains in winter,
In snowstorm and frostbite and wind.
With sleet slicing downward like splinters,
And the light leaving fast at day's end.

I love these dear mountains in autumn,
With aspens all burnished bright gold.
When the clouds curl so gently like cotton,
And the elk sing a story untold.

I love these dear mountains in summer,
With the wildflowers watching the trails,
Each blossom a welcome newcomer
Where the growth and the grace never fail.

I love these dear mountains in springtime,
When the snow first begins to retreat.
The earth then awakens to sing rhymes
Of a rebirth that cannot be beat.

I love these dear mountains the whole year,
In every season and clime,
And I will be loving them always,
From now till the end of all time.

September 26
I've been adopted by the High Peaks, where God has healed my soul and rechristened me again Vision and Dream.

BESIDE THE MEADOW
BLUE MOON

The rarest things in nature are the things we seldom see.
Perhaps a moth just crawling from cocoon upon a tree,
Or meteors that strike their sparks across the evening sky,
Or just-born elk calves wobbling brave with wonder-hungry eyes.
So many secrets hidden; just one look would not suffice—
Like a blue moon in the mountains,
Like lightning that strikes thrice.

The rarest things in life are the ones we see each day
But pass right by, not realizing the miracle they make.
Perhaps a parent's patience, or a joke told by a friend,
Or a love that keeps us hoping when all else is at its end.
Or the warmth of walking home, or a stranger's smile,
Or the grace that holds our hands through every weary mile.
So many gifts around us we never recognize—
Like a blue moon in the mountains,
Like lightning that strikes thrice.

HIGH COUNTRY HYMNAL
THINNER AIR

They say the air is thin here, but all I feel is healing flow through lungs taking their first deep breath.

They say the woods are danger, but insulation and isolation are devastation, and here I am safely unsafe.

They say the sun is scorching, but my eyes blink in the brightness and see through the shadows.

They say the mountains are called Rocky, but I feel through the grit of granite, down to the forging fires beneath, down to the slow warm throb of the earth's great heart.

They say the land is lonely, but I hear the Spirit still singing, the music that makes the mountains move, the peace like snowmelt rushing down into the wilderness, the love like a banner waving over my wandering way.

BESIDE THE MEADOW
MOOSE MUSE

He's long and he's strong and he's not as he seems;
He looks like a camel and horse had a dream.
His back humps up haughty, his nose droops demure;
He's wearing a rough rug that might pass for fur.

He's loud and he's proud since the day he was born,
And he's really impressed with his shovel-scoop horns.
See those sharp points? They're not just for show.
So you'd better be careful—don't make him your foe.

He's gruff and he'll bluff just 'cause he can;
His soul most resembles a grumpy old man.
He's ready to argue and ready to fight,
So give him a wide berth—but keep him in sight.

He's cool and he's full of talents so big.
The Natives once called him the "eater of twigs."
He can run like a racehorse and swim like a seal
Or even dive deep like a submarine eel.

He's rough and he's tough but he still shouts the praise
Of the One Who so lovingly shaped his weird ways.
Was he made to inform or just to amuse?
Either way, here he is: the masterpiece moose.

May 15
Moose are comic relief who take themselves so seriously!

BESIDE THE MEADOW
PIKA

A peek
And a squeak
And his nose gives a tweak—
The pika peers out from his home.
He's scared
But he's there
And he's ready to dare,
This elf of the mountain stones.

A flash
And a dash
And he darts to a cache—
Hiding there under the scree.
I look
In each nook
And in every crook,
But he's hidden away from me.

A puff
And a fluff
But surprisingly tough—
His home the most hostile of lands.
But round
He is found
Quite safe underground
And can fit in the palm of my hand.

HIGH COUNTRY HYMNAL

A nest
At its best
Just waiting for rest—
All snug when winter winds roar.
When snow
Finally goes
He'll be back in the show,
Ready to frolic once more.

BESIDE THE MEADOW
WHITE-COLLAR CAGE

Meetings that could have been emails,
Emails I wish I could forward,
Memos with too many details—
I'm getting dreadfully bored.
When streetlights are drowning the true stars,
I feel the wandering pull—
I'll slip through these white-collar cage bars
And go running wild through the woods.

Excel sheets that lose all their data,
Paperwork piling like snow,
Software that's clearly still beta,
Hear all of my civilized woes!
When workloads come lurching like landslides,
And I feel my soul smashing flat,
I know that I have to go outside,
The medicine I need is that.

Trading my life for a paycheck,
Far too many phone calls,
I haven't quite found a way yet
To prove these things matter at all.
And that's why I'll run to my homeland,
The mountains where I hope to stay,
Where God holds me close in His own hand,
And everything else fades away.

HIGH COUNTRY HYMNAL
THE ROCKIES IN THE FALL

Like a vein of precious ore, the golden aspens stripe the hill,
And the bugles of the bull elk ring through the morning chill.
The silver frost is sparkling; the trees are standing tall;
And I can't make up magic like the Rockies in the fall.

Like an arrow to the south, the wild geese pierce the sky,
And the sharpened winds are warning that winter's walk is nigh.
The pikas burrow bravely; the jays still rasp their call;
And I can't conjure courage like the Rockies in the fall.

Like a temple of His splendor, the mountains sing their praise,
And the leaves join in the chorus all through these painted days.
I'm laughing to the north wind, joy ringing through it all,
And I am wild with worship in the Rockies in the fall.

September 16
I'm home! Back in my mountains, in the fierce stark wildness of an untamed country where the air smells like courage and the sun shines freedom. The pines grip me with dark green fingers and lead me onward and upward.

HIGH COUNTRY HYMNAL
ELEPHANT HILLS

I am watching the lumpy swell of mountains against the horizon—
Wrinkled like the skin of the elephants that once held up the world,
Ridged like their bony uncomplaining shoulders.
Did those elephants ever tire?
But someone has to be the quiet one.
And given the choice,
Between accepting burdens or marching within a red tent,
I would choose as they did—to hold up the sky.

BESIDE THE MEADOW
BEAR PAW

"You can touch it." That's what the ranger
Said to this wide-eyed teen. I'd come across his truck
Where over the tailgate slung a sleeping bear,
Researchers drawing answers from his veins. I recall
That hovering smell of bear—like damp earth, strong skunk,
distant thunder—
The way the light teased
The glimmers from his fur, black as starless night. But
mostly I recall
The scars that crissed and crossed upon his paws,
Drawing constellations on his feet.
All years ago.
But still, some darker nights, I feel again
His paw against my palm—and I can see him
Shouldering still through many mountain secrets,
Walking a way not easy for any of us,
Following the scars and the stars to where he goes.

WITHIN THE FOREST

POEMS OF CONNECTION AND COMMUNITY

WITHIN THE FOREST
CAMO

You'll find me dressed in camo. All my life
I've loved the feel, the shape, the shadow.
The reddest head, the realest tree,
And I stand in the shade. And in the woods
From brush to bank I glide, hid in the hues
As if my body flicked before a screen,
Between the birthing beam and shifting image,
And suddenly I wore the movie. Some might say
That I wear these because I wish to hide,
Or just to spurn the way of this glass world.
And true it is that I have mouthed the bit
Of dry convention, the noose around the neck
Of all the world, politely petrified. And
True it is, that I have wished to hide.
Unsneered by mocking mouths, I'd run away
And nestle where the pines hold out their arms.
But really, if you ask me soft and steady,
And not with hidden bear-traps in each word,
I'll tell the truth. The mossy oak, the field and stream—
These are all my world. I wear the garb
To stitch myself within the land I love—
The spirit satisfied of every wooded hill,
Sororal kindred of each lap-leafed pinecone,
With all dry leaves of fall, November's kisses,
Tangled in my hair. You may not see me,
When I am wearing camo—but believe me:
The trees can see me, and I can see myself.

September 29
I sat on the big rock and closed my eyes, and in the waiting stillness all the land surged into me, and for just a moment the mountains and I were one.

WITHIN THE FOREST
FIRST HIKE

Is it easy? Oh, yes! It's a quite gentle climb.
Yes, of course we'll go slowly since it's your first time.
How far is it? Oh—perhaps three miles, or four.
Maybe a bit less. (But probably more.)
Watch your step there—oh! So you actually fell?
Yeah, that's how you learn to keep eyes on the trail.

Hotter today than they said it would be,
But heat can't stop hikers like you and like me.
I hope you brought plenty of water to drink—
What? Left it behind? But didn't you think?
Oh, hey—look right there. Do not step in that.
That's what is politely referred to as *scat*.

Now, this part right here is just slightly steep.
And don't lose your balance. That chasm is deep.
Is this not exciting? Aren't you having fun?
But why do you sound like you might burst a lung?
Oh, watch out for snakes, bears, and spooks. Yeah, they're real.
Have you heard of the disappeared man in these hills?

Well, look at that! Bear tracks, and pretty fresh, too.
Don't worry—he's probably not searching for you.
The view will be worth it, and—what's that you say?
Are we there yet? Well—um—we're almost halfway—
That's four miles up, one way—didn't I mention?
Oh—was an eight-miler not your intention?

HIGH COUNTRY HYMNAL

Now, the end is a rock scramble. Hold on real tight.
And—right there's the summit! A marvelous sight.
Well—the views aren't the best. It's too cloudy today.
But the joy's in the journey, now wouldn't you say?
All right. Catch your breath. That's not half bad, my friend.
Take photos, and now—we'll do all this again!

WITHIN THE FOREST
DIFFERENT, THEY CALLED ME

Different, they called me, said like a curse,
And most likely, out of my hearing, much worse.
I never could keep up with fashions and trends,
The movies and gossip that intrigued my "friends."
So I used to weep and feel like a fool,
But that was before I knew *different* was cool.

Unpopular I may have been to their band,
But a small price to pay for being known by my land.
The owls called a welcome, the trees were my friends,
I knew every curve of the creek where it bends.
All of my best days were spent in the woods—
Because I was learning that *different* was good.

I think of it now and can't help but take pity
On all of those folks who laughed in that city.
For they'll never sing the song of God's world,
Or see His High Country skies all unfurled.
They'll never laugh loud as they wrestle with wind,
And never run fearless all down to land's end.
And they'll never breathe courage on trails that stretch long—
Because hard as it may be, *different* makes strong.

I'm still known as *different* in my slice of earth,
And most folks still give me a pretty wide berth.
I'm still spinning stories, playing mainly with words,

HIGH COUNTRY HYMNAL

And I'm still most at home with the mountains and birds.
Different they called me, and *different* I'll stay—
I hope to be *different* till the end of my days.

WITHIN THE FOREST
MUSHROOM MIRACLE

For Lena, who looks for the light

Looking for mushrooms. Her text to me. Some photos alongside,
Snaps of them bouncing up like brave balloons from forest floor.
And then she spoke of *bioluminescence*—the word itself seems to glow,
The way she insisted these mushrooms would. Most folks, I'd doubt,
But I've seen her over and over unwrap reality, and show me a mystery inside.
So I believed in her, and she believed in them, and in the light they held.
Night after night, she waited, kneeling in the thick secret of an autumn dusk.
Still believing in the fire in the fungi—because that is like her.
She whose name means *light*—she finds it everywhere, mainly in the forgotten places,
Because she keeps believing after others walk away,
Because she never lets the dark have the last word.
What kind of God makes flashlights from fungi?
A good One, I'd say.
The same One Who makes her glow with grace.
All I know is, in my dark nights, she's still there—
Waiting patiently for the miracle that cannot be expected,
Coaxing forth the mystery that cannot be extinguished,
Believing in all the light in mushrooms, and in me.

September 16

What is it about this place? Whenever I am here, all is right and I feel as if I had never been anywhere else. I like who I am here. I am in the bright light— the Light that makes me cry!

WITHIN THE FOREST
MEET YOU IN THE MOUNTAINS

For Memaw, who saw so much

You never saw those rocky peaks that rise far to the west,
You spent your days in Arkansas, where every hill is less.
But still you knew of mountains, the strength and struggle too,
For you were always climbing hidden peaks I never knew.

You never saw the Milky Way within the starry sky,
As it swung across the Rockies, spilling all its light.
But still you knew of darkness, of nights so bleak and raw,
Yet you were always guided by a light I never saw.

You never heard the mountain winds murmuring their song,
And never knew the lyrics so that you could sing along.
But still you knew a melody, a song that drowned out fear,
And to that tune you followed, a song I didn't hear.

I've never seen the gates of gold that lie beyond the sun,
And never heard the worship rolling up before the Son.
The moment that you left us, the light burst in for you;
All disappointment died away, replaced by what is true.
So bright you're living now!—and I cannot wait to see;
I'll meet you in the mountains, and you'll be showing me.

HIGH COUNTRY HYMNAL
NO MAN'S LAND

I've seen the way you fight.
(You think I haven't noticed?)
I've watched the way you charge heart-strong into battle,
Smiling with your bloody knuckles, willing away your wounds.

And I've seen the way you fear.
(Of course I noticed.)
The way you try not to look over your shoulder,
The way you wait wary in the shadows, ready to run.

And I've seen the way you hide.
(Yes, I noticed that too.)
That concrete-and-Constantine wall around your heart.
You were tough because you had to be, until your courage calloused.
Being left for dead too many times can do that to a person,
Can leave you stitching barbed-wire borders like scars,
Can leave you living in an airless no-man's-land.

But I am calling to you across the trenches:
Let that land, too, belong to Him.
Let flowers grow in the foxholes.
Let grace wave in the wind over your war zone.
I cannot tell you that you will not be hurt.
But I can tell you that pain and love have always danced together.
I cannot tell you that you will not sink shell-shocked in

battle.
But I can tell you that this war has been won.
And I cannot tell you that no blood will be shed.
But I can tell you that blood has already bought yours,
That love is already waiting patiently beyond your walls,
That you can trust as fiercely as you fight—
You who stand on mighty mountains breathing the beginning,
You who hold His burning burst of glory in your heart,
You who will see His grace grow green along your crumbling walls.

November 22

I love this land. It is my home, my heart. Where else is the glory so pure, so undiluted? Where else can I stand on the crest of the wave of wonder?

WITHIN THE FOREST
THE EDGE OF IT ALL

I'll never forget her, sitting there,
All the weight of the cloudy sky upon her shoulders.
I won't forget the way her lips moved silently,
Talking only to empty air and waiting space and one farther away than both of those.
It wasn't until I saw the wind catch the ashes and swirl them away into the valley that I understood the tracks of her tears.
Brother. Cancer. Not enough life, not enough time, not enough—
The same sharp edges of the story of grief.
But he loved it here—pulling her coat tighter, gathering up the wind-whipped shreds of her strength, keeping her eyes on the peaks beyond us. *He wanted to come back here.*
She was sitting on the edge of the cliff, the brink of her emotions, and I was afraid to walk too close, to slip over that edge into something against which all my words weakened.
But I still remember my mother (afraid of heights, or so she always said)
Yet moving with steady feet over the jagged rocks,
Sitting on the edge of all that emptiness,
Her arms around the mourner she did not know.
I trust that one day, I'll have their courage—
The faith to fling what I cannot hold into eternity,
The love to weep with a stranger on the edge of all that none of us can know.

HIGH COUNTRY HYMNAL

LOVE AND DEATH AND EVERYTHING ELSE

He went missing in the fall, but they didn't find him till snowmelt,
Up on the mountain's frowning face, far above where the trees dare not trespass.
And that's his story: another sacrifice to a fourteener. From the valley, I can see the mountain that was his altar, and I draw back, a little.
How well do I really know these mountains, this land that has given me life and stolen it from another?
What makes me think that I'm their special favorite, that it won't be me someday pinned to a precipice?
I think on this for a couple of heartbeats,
Just long enough for a cloud to curl away across the meadow,
And then I'm lacing my hiking boots and I'm back out there.
My phone pings with a tear-stained text from my friend, all about the man she trusted
Against my better judgment—but can I, still making friends with the mountains, judge?
Strange, how the things we love can kill us,
Strange, how living without them would kill us anyway.

WITHIN THE FOREST
SHE WHO SENDS US CLIMBING

For Mama
Your mountains have been my making, your faith has been my foundation, your love has been my lifeline

They were flattened folk. Not their fault,
Just the way it was. Try it yourself—
Farming on the thankless prairie sod.
I wouldn't want to, not now, not then. So little wonder
That their hearts toughened as calloused as their hands,
That dreams became as dusty as the land,
That *practical* hemmed in whatever they planned.
I say this not to judge, but to explain. They did their job—
To hold the line, and live. But how glad I am
That my mother looked beyond with clearer eyes.
She left the land that pulled upon our blood, and forged her way
Westward into higher country, worshiping
The God of Whom she'd only seen the shadow, trusting
That He would lead her home.
And here she brought forth me—
Determined I would live in joy and pain,
Resolved my story would have a higher sky.
And here I am, a mountain girl, because she dared
To make me so. My children still
Will stand upon her shoulders,
She who shot our ancestral grit all full of grace,
She who sends us climbing higher even than she can see.

HIGH COUNTRY HYMNAL
EAGLE CANYON RAILWAY

For Dad, who follows the tracks

This is where the tracks run. Due west from here,
Eagle Canyon Railway. Can't you smell
Creosote's sharp pinch, feel the rumbling earth
Under the gallop of the Iron Horse? Look up.
Eagles, too big for sky, carving their circling way.
And there's the canyon—five hundred feet down.
See that? The tracks cross nothing here, but empty air, and trust.
How long? Who knows. Farther than we see.
And so, three-pronged decision at the canyon mouth: some folks
Turn themselves around, tear up their ticket,
Retreat back east where safety sings its siren song.
And some folks scramble up and down these hills
Looking for another way—but forward is always forged in fear.
(Hear that? It's closer now. Express in sixty seconds. Ring that bell.)
Where was I? Yes—the folks who choose to ride. The only ones
Who break into the borders. They keep their eyes
Not on the canyon, but on the cars; not on the trestle, but on the train,
Believing that all truth still holds those tracks,
Resolving that the journey will not fail,
Seeing past disaster, to the dream.

WITHIN THE FOREST

And here it is—train hot-churning, steel-snorting into station.
Take a ticket.
Ready to ride?

November 20
It's good to be here. When I saw the mountains rising today, I thought how very blessed I am—to have home always to return to.

WITHIN THE FOREST
ELK CALF

"*Unseasonable*" was the word they used, when the seasons slipped backwards and once more the snow swirled about the peaks.
The weather dragged its feet, steps behind the rest of nature's tempo. That must be why
I rounded the bend and saw them: the mother elk, hollowed by her efforts, and the barely-there baby that had just slid into the snow.
The mother was already standing, licking the young one, swiping off his stupor with insistent urgency.
And then he lurched up, camel-clumsy, back legs braced like tent stakes while front legs scrabbled hard—
A folding, like a paper bridge—the mother's urging—and then—there. He stood.
Before the triumph could tremble through his legs, she was leading him away,
Past us who'd gathered breathless, through the wraithful winds, into the arms of the mountain.
And it is always so, I think. Our children are born into a winter world that makes no special effort to welcome them.
No chance even to congratulate themselves on entering life,
Before life demands they run. No time to lie in the snow and freeze.
And all we can do
Is show them again and again how to stand,
And tell them to run before they know they are ready,
And point them toward the mountains higher than us all.

HIGH COUNTRY HYMNAL
TIMID TRUST

It is walking softly that does it. Trying to stir
As few ripples as possible in the waters of the world.
It is sinking into the stillness, wrapping into the waiting,
breathing in time with the heartbeat of the earth.
Then, the birds will fly to my fingers, steal seeds from my
patient palms.
Then, the bright bubbles of frog song will burst around me
again.
Then, the wild things will walk close enough to touch—once
they believe that I will not.
And I understand.
This is a world where belief is blown glass
And threads of trust can tangle. Only last night,
I sat on a friend's couch and spilled my story of sorrow,
My heart all sharp and shattered, fear fighting against the
rescue of release—
But her words were still as gentle as her heart.
So, this is what I want to say, to all the wild and wounded
just like me:
I will not reach before you are ready.
I will make no sudden movements.
I can be as still as the time unfolding around us, as soft as your
stammering story, as patient as the pattern that brought you here.
You are safe to take this terrifying trust from my hands.

WITHIN THE FOREST
MOOSE CHILD

Rocky Mountain autumn. Soft-smeared dusk.
Along the river, heavy-headed grass
Bows before the winter. Time to trust
That twilight too is tender. On the path
I see them—moose and calf within the brush.
The young one wide-eyed still, but growing fast
Into its eager world. And just downstream,
A baby toddles under parents' laughs,
Cameras clicking joy. Just two young things,
Together in a world in wonder cast.
And this, I think, is hope. And thus I pray,
For all the young ones in this world that's theirs to change—
> September secret beckons—carry it.
> The river still runs restless—bear with it.
> The wildness is your witness—care for it.
> This moment is your mystery—be there in it.
> The untamed earth awaits you—inherit it.

September 26
I love every trail and track in the park. But there is something special about being there, in the very High Country. The mountains are close enough to touch, there in the great heart of the peaks. Sweeping views and carved mountains and the exultation of all that is wild and free until I think my heart will break from the love of this my birthright.

WITHIN THE FOREST
THE KISSING BRIDGE

Meet me on the bridge, my love,
Where river kisses shore.
And there we'll stand
In this wild land
And seal our hearts once more.

Take me in your arms, my love,
When day blurs into night.
No depths so dark,
No shadows stark,
Could ever steal this light.

Kiss me one more time, my love,
Your name wraps into mine.
Our stories bound,
In you I'm found
From now throughout all time.

Promise me your heart, my love,
Just like this golden band.
A vow so deep
We've pledged to keep,
Witnessed by this land.

HIGH COUNTRY HYMNAL
BLACK LAKE LOVE

The eighth thing I love about you is that we still love,
Even on the days when the sun does not pull itself above the rim of Black Lake.
I whisper my fears into your silence,
And you absorb them with all the patience of the grayness before dawn.
When your hands begin to be heavy,
I stroke the muscles clenched like fists in your shoulders.
There is nothing in that inky lake that the sun will not see when it rises.
We break our hearts in halves—this love, like manna in the wilderness.

WITHIN THE FOREST
LEVI

Our trails intersected for the briefest moment,
Like lovers too shy to kiss. I remember very little.
Just how your voice held the laugh of the alpine streams,
How the sun struck gold against your hair,
How your eyes were clear, unclouded sky.
You asked my name. Once I remembered it, I told you.
And now I wish I hadn't been so busy
Trying to keep my tongue from tangling. Now I wish I'd asked you more,
Walked farther down the trail with you. But that's my life—
Busy dodging mistakes, I walk past miracles. You'd think I'd learn, sometime,
To chase the sparks, and let the fire burn.
But anyway,
I hope, one day,
Our trails might cross again.
This time I'll tell you more than just my name.
And all the way,
I wish you mountain paths all ripe for running,
The light that baptized you in brilliant joy,
And the wonder that opened your fearless eyes so wide.

HIGH COUNTRY HYMNAL
LOVE LIKE THE MOUNTAINS

I will want you to hold me like the mountains do,
In slow and steady arms, loving me
With the strength of a thousand years of granite grace.
I will want you to know me like the mountains do,
Walking with me along the scree-scraped trails of both our souls,
The backcountry beat of our hearts.
I will want you to laugh with me as the mountains do,
Cupping our hands around the fierce fire of joy,
Moments swirling like aspen leaves aflame.
I will want you to be as patient as the mountains are,
Still standing by me through all my wind-blown moments,
Ready to sling my sky across your shoulders and carry
Every sun and star of all my life with you.

ABOVE THE TREELINE

POEMS OF STRUGGLE AND STRENGTH

HIGH COUNTRY HYMNAL
tundra

I read the story once. In some poetry contest,
Where they pin prizes on paragraphs, his one-word poem:

tundra

And that was all. And of course the critics
Ran for their scalpels and started dissecting.
Is it a poem? Is it not? Could it have been?
I don't know what poetry is. Does anyone?
But all I know
Is that poetry is the art of seeing.
And when I read that word

tundra

I see that white and windswept world,
Where the gales race the clouds above the rafters of the mountains.
I see shadows of ravens spinning above the drifted white, and I see the pikas
Tucked amid the speckled stones.
I see the oversized sun, the mountains swelling like ocean waves all the way to Wyoming, the valleys that slope like the pitch of the roof to a ground deeper than I can see.
But mostly I see myself—
Lost in the wild white wonder of that lonely world,
Sung by the silence of an untamed land,

Shrunk back to proper size by a sky brimming over with a deep blue peace.

HIGH COUNTRY HYMNAL
GODFORSAKEN PLACE

Once I roamed in valleys green down by the riverside,
But now I've come to tundra cold where death itself is white.
My heart is freezing slowly; I cannot feel my face,
Here where I've been stranded in this godforsaken place.

The snow is silent judgment piling up on me,
And what I wouldn't give right now to see a single tree.
It isn't just the wind that smears these tears across my face,
Here where I've been stranded in this godforsaken place.

I don't know what I did to deserve this exile here,
Where every gust of wind resounds the wailing of my fear.
The silence now from Heaven is loud within this space,
In the empty stretches of this godforsaken place.

He said He'd never leave me, that His promises were true,
And I have tried to follow everything He said to do.
But for all of my obedience, He's left without a trace,
And my prayers are lifting lifeless in this godforsaken place.

But wait...

I know I serve a God Whose heart once froze upon a tree,
And I know that every tear I've cried, He's wept along with me.
And even in the tundra, brave flowers stretch for sun,

ABOVE THE TREELINE

And even broken trails have been mapped out by Someone.
The fact that I am breathing is still a mark of grace,
And perhaps there's no such thing as a godforsaken place.

HIGH COUNTRY HYMNAL
SANCTUARY

I have known what it is to run, panting like the prey, breath cracking ribs, heart wounding wild.
But there is still a refuge that wraps me like the circling charm of a rune.
Here is the hovering hush of the holy, silence that soaks up my striving.
Here are the wings that shadow me, the tenderness mightier than a mother's.
Here is the altar whose horns I grapple, the fire that burns but does not blister, the blood that cancels my curse.
Here is the Rock that is higher, the peace that is stranger, the Love that is greater, than all.

ABOVE THE TREELINE

October 13
I think of how many things were shattered—and yet God carefully held all those broken pieces in His palm and put me back together. I'll never stop exulting in His restoration!

HIGH COUNTRY HYMNAL
THE SHAPE OF GRACE

I have never known the shape of grace. I've always envisioned it beautiful,
Smiling sweetly like a mountain sunrise,
The blessing floating gently down on calm winds and fair skies.
But maybe, in all my cries and kicking, in all the ways I tangle in the story, I forgot to remember.
Maybe the face of grace is scarred and stern sometimes,
And maybe the answers that seem so hard are for the questions I did not know to ask.
And maybe when I splinter my fists against this iron door—
Maybe it is grace that fit the lock,
And grace that steels His tender heart against my pleas,
Determined to give me not what I think I want,
But what I do not know I need.
It is grace, sometimes, that widens my trail and calms my winds.
But it is still grace—the rude, relentless kind—that stands before me with a flaming sword.

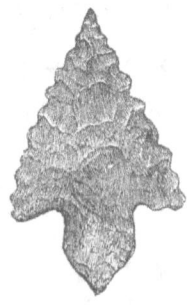

ABOVE THE TREELINE
GLACIER GLORY

It's not an easy birth when mountains rise.
First there was the flat, the land unscarred.
And then God chose His chisel, and went to work.
Complacency gave way to cold, and ice spread south,
Relentless as redemption.
A thousand years of freezing/forging, shaking/shearing—
Great groaning glaciers pulling forth the peaks.
And then—the High Country, born from winter's womb.
Who knew that birth could be so brutal?
But I too have lived
Forgetful in my flatness, until His ice
Scraped within my soul, to raise
Topography of triumph. He takes me higher
Than I would take myself. Becoming is not bloodless,
And *good* is much too pure to hold no pain.
But when His work is done, and glaciers melt,
The mountains stand—
A strength that would not come without the struggle,
A grace that would not come without the groaning,
A story that would not sing without the scar.

October 8
I fell in love with Jesus, dancing with Him across His High Peaks.

ABOVE THE TREELINE

MISSING MOUNTAINS

The wind came up. The fog fell down. And they were gone.
Those mighty mountains carved against the western sky—
invisible.
Like curses cast by spiteful spirits, clouds erased
Those gentle granite giants—all the world
Muted now in monotone, horizons hemmed.

Yes, I've seen foggy days. And every time,
I drift into despair, almost convinced
That all I trust has vanished, sealed behind
Every cursed cloud. But how can I forget?
The mountains stand forever with a song
That can't be shrunk with silence. No flimsy fog
Can ever shake what's true. And so I smile
Because I know the way of west,
And still behind the storm, my mountains stand.

HIGH COUNTRY HYMNAL
AFTER THE FIRE

Sorry it's so ugly. That's what she said, just like that,
Scowling at the blackened footprint of the wildfire,
As though the scarred and saddened land was to blame.
The sting of her sentence went into me too, and what I really wanted to do
Was take the shame-faced mountains into my arms, and sing them this song:
Yes, you are scarred, but so am I.
I know what fire is, and how it feels
As it wracks my heart in pyrotechnic pain,
Turning all my sureness into smoke, and passing by,
Leaving a wasteland in its wake. I know how these mountains feel.
I too wept and believed all beauty lost. But who is to say?
What if endurance carries its own loveliness?
What if new life is ready to burst forth with the joy of the morning,
Stirring like a beautiful secret within this ground
Where the ashes make the soil rich and ready?

ABOVE THE TREELINE

THINGS TO DO WHEN YOUR WORLD ENDS
(incomplete list)

1. Leave the shattered pieces where they are. Let the light catch on the broken glass, but you do not have to be grateful for it yet.

2. Call friends who are not afraid of sharp edges. Show them the wounds that must be stitched back to safety. Trust that you are loved more than you were admired.

3. You may sob, sing, or swear, as long as all of it is unflinchingly honest prayer.

4. Get up and wash your face and walk outside. See that the stars have not stepped off their paths. Hear that the wind is still bringing in the new. Remember that the flowers will unhurriedly weave their worship for a thousand more years, and the throne farther north than north itself is not unoccupied.

5. Fill a bird feeder. Heap up the bursting seeds in handfuls. Watch as the songbirds swoop in—the ones who are still trusting, still hoping, still rejoicing without questions in the good that came without their striving, the good that was provided by wounded hands in unexpected grace.

HIGH COUNTRY HYMNAL
KRUMMHOLZ

These are the trees that grow on the edge of the possible,
Their roots the teeth of tenacity into this rock.
This is where forest fades and sky swoops in.
The story is scarred in their forms—
The roots all reaching for some welcome from the earth,
The branches all clinging like crooked fingers to the clouds,
The trunks all warped by wind, and weather, and waiting.
I know this story too. I've lived my life
As a song sung stubborn—dug in determined,
Here where my roots reach relentless. They've shaped me too,
All the things that strain and stretch a soul.
A bit misshapen, maybe?
But—here I am.
I too have learned to grow within the wind,
I too have learned to call the clouds by name.

(A German word meaning "crooked wood," *krummholz* refers to the gnarled and miniaturized trees that grow on the treeline— the stark edge where the forest meets the tundra. These wind-twisted trees carry the same beautiful bravery that works in our souls when we too grow in our given grace.)

May 21
O El Shaddai! I'm here again! I'm caressed by Your winds, on the steep shoulders of Your High Places, bathed in Your love. I'm alive, and here I am well, I am whole!

HIGH COUNTRY HYMNAL
SNOW

Is this not how grace comes—a silent surprise,
From a Heaven we both hoped and feared had forgotten us?
Is it not always like this, a million relentless miracles,
Each landing like a kiss on the undeserving barrenness of winter ground?
How soft it is, how quiet, pulling peace like a quilt over the world,
Soothing all our strivings into rest.
But how strong it is, enough to cover everything—
A purity we didn't have to pay for,
A holiness we didn't know to hope for,
A love we can only live for.

ABOVE THE TREELINE
DAY AND NIGHT

"For he wounds, but he binds up; he shatters, but his hands heal." — Job 5:18

He's God of the day and He's God of the night,
He's a deep smoky dark and a pillar of light.
He laughs in the joy of a blazing high noon,
He mutters His mysteries in the dark of the moon.

He carefully nurtures each delicate seed,
Then blasts forth His lightning and shivers the tree.
He rages like fire, He soothes like spring rain,
He judges His people, then revives us again.

Some days I can bask in the warmth of His smile,
Some days I have doubts if I'm even His child.
He's taken my dreams and He's wrecked all my plans,
But still He has lavished His love where I stand.

The Wonderful One—by this Name He is known,
With thoughts that are higher by far than my own.
Perhaps only miracles come from His hand.
Perhaps all is grace…and I need not understand.

For I don't want a God I can hold in my hand,
I don't want a deity I can command.
If I can't even fathom the depths of my mind,
Why would I want His thoughts smaller than mine?

HIGH COUNTRY HYMNAL

If He's a pillar of fire, I'll dance in the light;
If He's hidden in storm clouds, I will walk not by sight.
I only can hope to glimpse parts of His ways,
Yet still I will follow for all of my days.

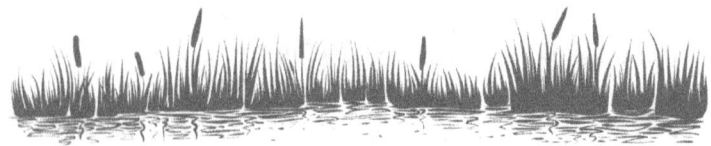

ABOVE THE TREELINE

September 20

It was wonderful, the periwinkle dust of dusk filtering down. The wind blew in a crash from Longs Peak, as the summit gleamed noble in the twilight. I shivered in the cold but stood in throbbing raptured awe, breathing broken words of love to my Lord Who rides upon the whirlwinds.

HIGH COUNTRY HYMNAL
HOW CAN I HELP BUT SING?

What though the road should wind weary,
And the dull-drumming days should stretch long?
What though the clouds should droop dreary,
And the battle belong to the strong?
What though my heart is all ragged
From the thorns that are bloody to pierce?
What though my mountains are jagged,
And the wind howls ferociously fierce?
What though all friends should abandon
And I must walk onward alone?
What though there's no hope to land on,
And every face is a stone?
Still in the midst of the mountains
The Lord of all hosts is my shield;
Still His great love is a fountain,
A river that flows through green fields.
And still in His grace I am living;
His smile is above everything!
And still that grace He keeps on giving—
So how can I help but sing?

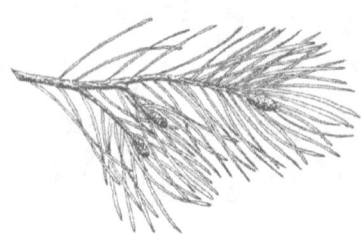

ALONG THE RIDGE

POEMS OF TRAILS AND TRUST

HIGH COUNTRY HYMNAL
LEAD ME FORTH

Gentle Savior, in these wilds,
Watch with love Your helpless child.
As I walk this lonely land,
Keep me clinging to Your hand.
The woods are rough, with dangers filled—
Faithful Jesus, be my shield.

Guiding Spirit, be my North,
Unchanging star to lead me forth.
Maps may muddle, paths may lie,
Only You can point me right.
Arrogance is but a trap—
Holy Spirit, be my map.

God of mountains, You Who wait
Over the horizon's gate—
May every trail lead back to You,
My place of rest when journey's through.
One day these hills I'll no more roam—
Father, be my welcome home.

September 29

I looked at the sparkling lake and the peaks smiling at me, and I asked God for courage, for fierce following Him in the days ahead. And I cried, because I love this place, and its God, so much. And it was all silver shadowed in the five-o'-clock light, and eternity replaced time and peace erased all fear.

HIGH COUNTRY HYMNAL
MOUNTAIN BROOK

I hope I can dwell like a mountain brook
In the place where it begins—
A bubbling thing from a hidden spring,
Joy arising again.

I hope I can sing like a mountain brook,
That speaks its splashing praise;
The stones all hear the song so clear,
This canticle of grace.

I hope I can wait like a mountain brook,
All patient in the freeze.
From winter's grip till spring's first drip,
It sleeps beneath the trees.

I hope I can dare like a mountain brook
With faith enough to leap.
With a mighty splash and a roaring crash,
It jumps fearless to the deep.

I hope I can live like a mountain brook
That knows its watery way.
Poured from His hands across this land,
To return to the ocean someday.

ALONG THE RIDGE
EL SHADDAI

You're the alpenglow that lingers
When my soul is growing dark;
You're the sun slipped through my fingers,
You're the silence and the spark.
You are fragrant like the pine trees,
You are spacious like the sky,
You're the Lord Who guides me kindly—
My God, my El Shaddai.

You're the Rock that leads me higher,
Up where the mountains cure.
You're the purging truth of fire,
You're the flowing fountains pure.
You are more than I can dream of,
You, the King Who reigns on high,
I'm buoyant in this deep love—
My God, my El Shaddai.

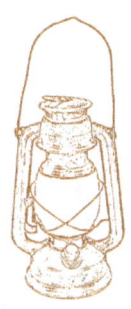

HIGH COUNTRY HYMNAL
TRUE NORTH

You Who inhabits the sides of the north,
Lord, like a compass, be leading me forth.
So many trails in a tangling maze,
Only Your guidance can make plain my ways.

How many times do we flounder and fail,
Twisting your truth to fit our crooked trails;
But even when we try redrawing the lines,
Your finger points north in a standard sublime.

God Who has stretched out the east and the west,
Be now the Polestar, and lead me to rest.
Pull me magnetic wherever I roam,
And at last, O True North, see me safe home.

November 27
"These are so your mountains," Mom said earnestly tonight, and she's right. I was thinking today, as I watched them against the horizon while we left, how different my life would have been had we not come back here. The mountains have been the anvil against which El Shaddai has shaped my life, and I'm so grateful.

HIGH COUNTRY HYMNAL
OUZEL

Submerged in shallow streams,
He picks his watery way
On submarine trails.
Again and again he peers underneath the surface for
something only he can see.
I want to be a dipping bird,
Walking in waters too deep for me alone,
Baptizing myself over and over again in the redemptive rush
of the River.

(The American Dipper, also known as the "water ouzel," is North America's only aquatic songbird. This brave and special bird literally walks underwater, picking its path along the beds of alpine streams to feed on insects and small fish. The ouzel reminds me to leave the comfort of my own shallows and instead forge fearlessly into the depths.)

ALONG THE RIDGE
SONG OF THE STORM

It's first the wind that rushes down, at once both sharp and sweet,
Electric with the incense that rises from these peaks;
It's then the clouds come tumbling, as of the wind they're born;
I'm standing on these mountains, unready for the storm.
And to the untamed God my prayers now I will offer up,
As the rain comes spilling from His overflowing cup.

And then the storm is on me, and the beast of thunder growls,
He shakes the rocks and twists the trees and makes the winds to howl.
The echoes of his fury shake me to my very core,
I'm hidden in this hollow rock—I dare not ask for more.
And to the untamed God my praises I won't fail to cry,
As the blinding blare of lightning finally splits the stormy sky.

And then the wind grows weaker; the hail no longer pounds,
And then the storm has swept away just like a swishing gown.
Each raindrop lifts its face to catch the sun's returning glow,
And there against the blue sky splash the colors of His bow.
And to the untamed God my thanks I'll sing across this land,
For even in the storm clouds, I was always in His hand.

HIGH COUNTRY HYMNAL
ALPENGLOW

I've seen it in the mornings. I have stood
In nights still dripping dark, no hint of sun,
And then the sky blooms pink, a sacred song,
And all the light's just there. It's strangely soft,
RSVP from daylight, a promise kept
Before the sun appears.

And I've seen it in the evenings. Blurry edge
As dusk smears day away, there it is.
A last long glow, a slow *good night*,
Along the western world—as if the sun
Is urging all the earth to not forget,
To watch for day again.

I've seen it, and I love it. And this same light
That cradles close the land has held my heart.
In all my soul's dark corners, I've seen the glow,
The promise that the light will still break through,
Sacred surprise. Then I can walk
With courage under any starless sky,
And hold that lingering light.

October 19
I am blessed of mortals, for no matter what befalls, the crystal light of Heaven breathes round about me. And I know what color the aspens are in the High Country of the Rockies.

HIGH COUNTRY HYMNAL
TO THE UNTAMED GOD

They told me just what size You are,
As if You're their specimen, pinned to a card;
Pound for pound, and gram for gram:
A God to carry with one hand.

> But I have felt the weight of glory,
> And the weightless brush of butterfly wings,
> And the awe draped over my shoulders.

They told me just how far You reach,
Your frontiers marked from west to east.
The limits laid, the maps all made:
A God to keep within a cage.

> But I have seen the clouds unrolling free across the sky,
> The light that bursts a million miles from any star,
> The hope that finds my heart in secret song.

They told me just how safe You stand,
Your power given with no demands.
A three-letter Name, so easy to hear:
A God to come to without fear.

> But I have heard the music of Your mystery,
> The swinging spheres sing in the hidden face of night,
> The thunder crackles from the unutterable Name.

ALONG THE RIDGE

They told me just how simple Your grace,
Spiritual science, formulae of faith.
1-2-3, the rules that bind:
A God to hold within my mind.
> But I have seen You break each law,
> The sizzling lightning rips the night,
> And still You shock me upside-down.

They argue in their lab coats still,
Shrink You down to fit their bill,
Shunning Shekinah, where You reside,
Dissecting divinity upon their slides.
> But I know Who You are, and I worship You as You are:
>> Untamed, undiluted, unabridged, unexplained—
>> The God Who is more than we'll ever know,
>> The God Who is wilder than all that we are,
>> The God Who flings farther than we'll ever go,
>> The God Who is drawing me into His heart.

HIGH COUNTRY HYMNAL
OLYMPUS

The old gods demanded that we humans climb
The slopes of Olympus to reach the sublime.
No help could we ask from the deities there,
Who never pretended to love or to care.
We offered up all to ward off their wrath,
Only to watch them consume us at last.
Hopeless perfection insisted by all,
But all of us slip—into darkness we fall.

Yet when my God was raising the heads of the peaks,
He already knew that our dust was weak.
He loved us too much to leave us alone,
So He came down the mountain to lead us back home.
He took on Himself our own form, and then
Died in the valley to pay for our sin.
Now His grace is our song, and we are His prize,
Finally free—into glory we rise.

June 3

We were <u>in</u> the High Country—truly in it, of it, embraced by it. The cooling, cleansing fire of the High Peaks was in me, the spirited ruggedness of Mills Lake was before me, and the hand of my God was upon me. It was life!

HIGH COUNTRY HYMNAL
PROLOGUE

What if winter's sharp shadows were only
The prelude that comes before spring?
What if these lonely nights only whispered
Of the light that the dawning will bring?
What if every hard fall only signaled
That we would be rising again?
What if every bleak end simply told us
That something new soon would begin?
What if all of our tears would be counted
And weighed back in joy without bounds?
What if losing our way wasn't final
And just meant that we could be found?
What if death itself is but the doorway
To a world where all things are well?
What if all of this life is the prologue
To the story that Heaven will tell?

ALONG THE RIDGE
ENDING AND BEGINNING

One day the stars will shred the sky in retributive rain,
Like memories the mountains high will melt into the plain,
The hills will crumble 'neath the weight of all the toppling trees,
And fiery tongues will lick the last of every sizzling sea.
The firmament will flame and fume around the gasping sun,
And it will be the ending—creation all undone.

That day, I'll see horizons vast all gathered like a scroll
As the Author pens the ending to the story that's been told.
But when what's made has vanished, then I'll see the Maker's face,
From the threshold of a dying world, I'll step into His grace.
From forever to forever we'll cry glory to the Son,
And it will be the restart—creation all begun.

HIGH COUNTRY HYMNAL
TABERNACLE

Holy, holy, holy—
Concentric rings of glory—
Gentiles court, then shewbread laid, then Ark with flaming swords.
Sacred's at the center
Beyond the reach of sinners
Peripheral, I'm pleading for the Presence of the Lord.

Holy, holy, holy—
Layers build on glory—
Valley green, then mountain woods, then treeline and above.
I find Him in His dwelling
The earth His love is telling
Liberal, He overflows the world with all His love.

Holy, holy, holy—
Now I know Him fully—
The heavens of the heavens still cannot contain His grace.
Galaxies can't hold Him
Yet He makes my soul His homeland
Centripetal, I'm shouting forth: He's worthy of all praise.

September 21

I wish I had words to write what's slowly mending my war-torn heart, but I can't. I can only know it and feel it, feel myself becoming strong and free and well.

HIGH COUNTRY HYMNAL
RECLAIMED

Last year it was all the cloud of dust and choke of exhaust, thick-ribbed tires rutting and roaring between the broken teeth of the old mining pit. The land gaped wide and ugly like a wound not allowed to heal.

But this year the new levees embraced the blue promise of water and the grass grew delirious in the twice-turned dirt. Even the diving ducks have returned, each one flashing beneath the water like an offense forgiven.

Reclaimed is how they described the change to me, and that is a word I love.

Once I too wallowed, wounded, in the dust, my pain howling to the sky. And then scarred hands wrapped me securely like the levees. Hands that still saw purpose, still saw what my mud-mired soul could be. Hands with the patience of the lake water and the persistence of the grass and the relentless courage of the birds.

Reclaimed.

I watch this land shimmer under the glory of that word, and I walk with it stamped on my heart like a seal, and meanwhile in the dust of this world He is still making all things new.

BEYOND THE HORIZON

POEMS OF FAITH AND FOREVER

HIGH COUNTRY HYMNAL
INVERSION

I was only driving home. Another day
Of winter treading hard on autumn's heels.
Some chilly fog, some slapping wind, and I
Was only marking time. And then—inversion.
Ahead of me
The mountains were replaced by curling clouds,
Themselves all swirled and stacked like mountains too,
As if a window opened to a realm,
Of which earth's wonders are a shadow pale.
Reality is mostly unexpected.
I laughed, for fairytales are always preaching
"long ago and far away"—but now and here the wonder waits,
In this world where autumn whirls all wild,
And mountains morph from stone to cloud,
And I pull off the road and gape at what I never thought,
My expectations all subverted and inverted,
As they need to be.

BEYOND THE HORIZON
CANYON ROAD

The road is a clever one. Determined to meet the mountains, it first comes sideways,
Across the sleeping swell of foothill pastures
Right to the canyon. You think, watching, that there's no way,
That it's dead-ending right into the folded arms of stone.
Then
Suddenly
So curving
So
Narrow
It rushes right through the rift in the rocks,
Finding a gateway you'd never notice. From there the rest is not easy, but simple.
Courageous crisscrossing up the galloping ground,
Driving past the glowering granite walls until suddenly the horizon flings open arms, and I'm back in my mountain home.

I think of that road often.
I remember it when I too stand before my fears,
The sneering stone that wants to wall me in, to trap me in this lowland.
Not this time, because
I see that gasping gap. Just wide enough to walk through, if I will.
And I can picture what the road is like on the other side, how it will lead me first

HIGH COUNTRY HYMNAL

Into the chaos of the canyon—but then,
If I follow, upward,
Through the squeezing grip of every lie
And finally where the mountains rise at last.
You know—I think I'm ready for the trip.
I picture myself driving it,
Foot eager on the gas, radio loud, smile easy,
Plunging, laughing, into the canyon of everything I ran from,
Finding all the joy I long for on the other side of fear.

November 23
I drove us through the canyon to Estes Park—there was a strange and beautiful exhilaration in the cold and the snow and the whole wild dance of the winter mountains.

HIGH COUNTRY HYMNAL
ENTERING HEAVEN

No, I do not think I will see you on some overstuffed cloud in the sky.

And God knows you are not really a gown-and-harp sort of person.

So this, then, is how it will be—

Right after I slosh up out of the river, the glittering mountain will rise before me,

All purple heather and gold-grace grass and sunlight dreaming over the valleys.

I will see the city at the top, flinging forth the Light that is more than light—and I will run,

Run with the fierce fire-breathing joy, the power of a wild heart made well.

You will race out to meet me, and I will see you coming, and this is how I know there will be tears even in Heaven.

And hand in hand we will run together into forever, into the Light that dissolved all darkness, into the Love that has made us both people of the mountain.

BEYOND THE HORIZON
LAKE OF DREAMS

Here in the mountains' quiet cool,
Is tucked the Lake of Dreams.
It's hidden in this valley still,
Where nothing's as it seems.

I was a small child when I came here before. I marched right in, ducking past the outstretched hands of the pine trees with the intrepid trespass of clear-eyed children. I stood in the circling citadel of these mountains and looked, as I do now, on the Lake of Dreams.

I asked for nothing then—no need, when I believed that dreams were plentiful things. Like the smooth stones of the lakeshore. Just find one that felt good in my hand, I thought. No need to scribble my questions across the vermilion lake that rested like a shimmering emerald in the necklace of the woods. No need to listen for answers in the gentle murmur of the waters on the rocks.

So I shrugged at the sacred shores and headed down the mountain to do my own growing up and falling down and everything in between.

But now—now I am back, and I am afraid. I have seen the eruptive, disruptive power of dreams. I have seen them cast bat-wing shadows and become nightmares. And I have seen them melt into white-stag wishes that drag us exhausted through the woods.

No way to see the depth of this lake. Not now, when the water is just as clear, but my eyes are far less so. Somehow I think vaguely of King Arthur's legend, the one I always found unsettling. A hesitating knight, and an unknown arm brandishing Excalibur. Dreams are like that. Priceless. Piercing. And, at least the best ones, painful.

I did not know if I had the courage to come. Now I know I do not have the courage to leave. Fish slip through the grassy fringes of the water like missed opportunities, but the lake's invitation still stands. I'm half asleep now. Or maybe half awake. I dive—sliding into the enchanted green heart of the Lake, reaching farther than my arms can remember, stretching in the darkness for the dream that will pulse with the power of these hills and draw me back to the light.

"Dream on," cynics sneered.

I think I will.

BEYOND THE HORIZON
HEART OF THE MOUNTAINS

There are places so deep in these mountains,
Too deep for adventure to find,
Where silence suspends like a cobweb,
And nature obeys outside time.
A thousand springs' worth of wildflowers
Have reached to the sky all unknown,
And rocks that were hewn by the Ice Age
Are still stacked up stone upon stone.
The trees that fall deep in that forest
Have no one to muse about sound,
And the myths written deep in these mountains
Are those that will never be found.
Yet the Maker of Mountains is watching,
Not turning His love or His gaze—
And there, all alone with the Artist,
The heart of the mountains gives praise.

May 21
I breathe Your grace, Lord, I hear Your laughter, and I slough off the darkness and fear and isolation like filthy rags. Why seek the living among the dead?—and here I am alive in You as I never can be quite as fully anywhere else. These mountains, my Thin Place, are Your High Country.

BEYOND THE HORIZON
CONTINENTAL DIVIDE

I have balanced on the backbone of a continent, where God
is still parting the waters as they fall.
And I know what science says, all about the water's way—
A little more west: Big Sur curving across the ancient hills,
and the widespread hands of the palm trees, and the
breathtaking blue of the Pacific drinking up the sky.
A little more east: cold Atlantic waters of shipwrecks and
secrets, and the breakers that fall headlong upon the barrier
islands, and the fishermen in their squeaky wet boots hauling
lobster traps upon the coasts of Maine.
Or so I've heard it said. But all I can think
Is how this God Who parts the waters with His hands
Has given me my own divides. How many times I've stood
Upon the knife-edge of a single choice!
So how close have I been, over and over,
To veering off a continent away from all the stars?
And how many hairbreadth happenings, over and over,
Have led me to the right side of the rocks?
I, who can't feel the wind from a butterfly's wings, do not
see His hand. So I don't know.
And I don't know, even now, where I am going.
But I make my choices the same way the water does:
trusting the rivers that thread like a roadmap through the
wilderness.
I'll smell the salt when I get there.

HIGH COUNTRY HYMNAL
AUTUMN LAKE

The lake waits patiently, all its heart stretched open.
On this unexpectedly sunny day, right here at the last of autumn, the water has drunk the sky right into itself.
The reflections watch each other, clouds above and below me keeping company.
The light ripples off the water onto the tree trunks, drawing us all into the dance.
The sun is warm, the wind is chilly, but at least I am feeling something, at least the chalky dirt beneath my feet is firmer than I had feared.
When did I let myself forget to know what the tangled tongues of the cattails are murmuring to the wind?
Far above and behind me, at the very edge of my knowing, the red-tailed hawk hurls his cry into the clouds.
I will wait here as long as it takes,
Until I too can find the firm ground,
Until I too can brandish the war whoop,
Until I too can soak up the sky.

BEYOND THE HORIZON
ETERNITY

I'm as surprised as you, that God insists
We're creatures of eternity—we whose wrists
Are strapped with ticking clocks, a ball and chain,
So that we chafe impatient and insane.
Mesmerized by instant gratification,
We spend our days in mindless stupefaction.
Instant coffee, red-light rage, expressway—
And yet a timeless God still calls our names.
We're settling for seconds. His fresh-brewed grace
Still brims unhurried within each day.
Maybe that's the purpose of this earth,
To teach us that each death is just a birth;
Perhaps it takes us all these fragile years
To learn His timeless tune beyond our fears.
Perhaps time should be sown instead of spent.
We'll learn to live in that ascent
When we can see a kingdom as a page,
And a trembling flower's bloom a lingering age.

September 25

At The Loch today, I was watching the sun dance on the water and looking at the glacier that's huddled in its cirque for thousands of years. And suddenly, I was just overcome with the <u>bigness</u> of it all—the vastness in time as well as space. I just stood there and let the holy hugeness overshadow me, and remembered that as small as I am, the Author smiles on me with love.

BEYOND THE HORIZON
SHEEP LAKES

Timid is the word. You can't believe
Just how soft they step. We see these curled-horn rams
As the snorting red-rough mighty mascots; but really
Fear is what they take, not what they give. They hold those horns
On uncertain heads, with trembling legs, and velvet lips, and soundless hooves,
Walking the knife-edge between cliff and courage, safe among the secrets of the rocks.
But I have seen them come
Out of the mountain stronghold, down to the valley low, and cross the busy road just to reach
The salts that bake along the mineral flats. I always squeeze sweaty palms in sympathy
When the quiet creatures flinch as cars shove by—and I hold my breath in hope,
Until the fear cools into courage, until their dainty hooves
Clatter out a chorus on the pavement, and the salt's in sight. I don't know
What it is that moves me; but all I hope is this:
That I too can stand on the fringe of all my fear
And listen not to the tune of terror, but instead
To that strong and steady voice that calls from the other side.

HIGH COUNTRY HYMNAL
NEVER SUMMER

They call it Never Summer. The winter waits
Within these walls of wilderness. No smile of sun
Could ever thaw the snows stored safely here.
I've looked across the tundra's roof and seen it,
The jagged turrets of the silent stronghold,
Where the mountains hold so closely all they know.
These rocks remember everything:
The great and groaning glaciers, the stubborn snow,
The ice that cracked a continent, and made the mountains rise.
The ice has melted now, but not yet here.
Here, the mountains guard the ancient tales.
Here, they hold that silent heart of ice—
The winter that will never be forgotten,
The summer that will never fully come.

BEYOND THE HORIZON
STORM PASS
10,250 feet elevation

I started in the valley. Far below,
It's sunlit, sleeping, snug in all it never has to know.
Fine, for it. But as for me,
I'm climbing higher, following the promise dropped
Like an aspen leaf. Longs and Meeker
Watch me with their ancient patience. Cloud shadows show
The shape of what's to come:
Cumulonimbus.
Already, sky scuds silver; thunder rattles
Down the scree-stacked slopes. But I've shaken hands,
Sworn to fall as best I can
Upon the side of trust. I'll drink the rain,
Pull every pulse of power from the lightning.
And in this pause between the peaks, may I be found
Faithful, waiting for one whispered word.
Safer trails exist; I'd rather stand
Here, where the God of whirlwinds takes my hand;
Here, where the crackling onward dares me forth;
Here, upon the shoulders of a storm.

September 20
Tromping across the moraine where the rocks still sing of a frozen time, and the peaks raise praise in an awe that steals my soul—well, it settles all the things in me that otherwise grow hard and heavy, and it cures me of my recurring tendency to presume that I understand El Shaddai. How mysterious is the light that cracks the darkness in a million subtle ways!

BEYOND THE HORIZON
NOVEMBER PRAYER

The year is sinking low, and now these trees
That flamed so high in triumph turn to ash.
Leaves like pages flutter down; the story's told,
And winter ends the chapter. But here I am,
At the end of all You wrote this year. My leaves fell too,
But even in this two-toned world, the sky is startling blue.
I am glad that You are still writing. November never has the final word.
And in the year to come, let me be scribbled with Your sentences—
You Who are the Word—
As You are always writing, may I be always reading,
Finding Your signature in the awful and awe-full days.

HIGH COUNTRY HYMNAL
WALKING WEST

I will be walking west all my life. I will come here
Until I have learned the land like a dance I do not lead.
Until I have mastered the intricate steps:

> How to catch the clouds on my shoulders and ripple through the rain.
> How to let the light in without fear and kindle the alpenglow against the night.
> How to rise on hawk wings and carve circles over the ground-bound.
> How to stand with patient peaks and trust the long slow knowing of eternity.
> And before all, how to cup courage in my hands and hold fearless face to the west.

But until then,
Until false steps no longer dim the dance,
I will come here, to the place of power, the gate of glory,
Soul catching sun like a prism,
Heart leaping high like a pine,
Spirit pointing skyward like a peak who trusts the granite below and the grace above.

BEYOND THE HORIZON
BIRTHDAY CANDLES

Another mountain autumn. Cloud-curls shed confetti,
And silver frost is wrapping every tree in ribbons. Another year
Is layered on my face. I am a tree,
Adding rings each season, and I fight
To keep my skin from growing hard, to keep the green
Still dripping in my heart. But all around
My mountains raise their changeless faces.
Aspens glow like birthday candles, waiting for the wind
To puff them out in winter's wish—but until then
They'll race that flame beyond each stony peak. Those same sparks glow
Within my still-green soul, to burn more bold
With each unspooling year. So here I stand,
Within my peaks in autumn's slant. I will be here
Until the green glows out,
Until the seasons change,
Until those sparks shatter into the sky.

November 24

This is my grateful heart, thanks brimming over—I am home in my mountains. I _do_ know where I belong, and I will return and return and return. I am a mountain girl. And best of all, best by far, the God of the mountains—my wild and raw and fierce El Shaddai—calls me His.

BEYOND THE HORIZON
HIGH COUNTRY BLESSING

May you receive the blessing of the hard and holy way,
Other paths are easier, but they won't so richly pay.
May your trails be long and winding, may your mountains ever be steep,
May El Shaddai be with you as He guards your soul to keep.

May the rivers that you ford have currents swift and strong,
But may you still find beauty in the rhythm of their song.
May your nights be sometimes starless, your days sometimes too bleak,
May El Shaddai be with you as His holy face you seek.

May your paths be often lonely, may your company be few,
But may the ones who walk the road be faithful friends and true.
May you stand against the giants, hold conviction like a stone,
May El Shaddai be with you, for you know you're not alone.

May you learn to make your sunshine, even in the rain,
May you always feel the triumph of pushing through the pain.
May you hold the hope of springtime even in the snow,
May El Shaddai be with you—joy will blossom as you go.

I know you want an easy path; God knows I want it too,
But it's only climbing mountains that leads us to the view.

HIGH COUNTRY HYMNAL

And so I pray most earnestly that you won't cheat yourself—
May you live the epic story only faithfulness can tell.
So may you laugh with courage in the face of every wind—
The God of mountains is your strength—go in grace, my friend!

THANK YOU!

Thank you so much, friend, for joining me on this journey! I hope that you found peace, presence, and perspective in these pages.

I'd also like to ask you for a kind favor—if you enjoyed this book, would you mind leaving a rating or review for it on your preferred retail site? Reviews are an enormous help to authors, and they're also the best way for other readers to find books they'll love. Thank you in advance!

Now, before you go, I'd like to share one last thought.

I was born and raised on the shoulders of Arkansas's Ouachita Mountains—rolling hills that are beautiful, to be sure, but only a thousand feet above sea level at the highest point. But when I was twenty, my family traveled to Estes Park, Colorado, and I immediately lost my heart to the High Country.

It's fascinating to me now, looking back, how the mountains transformed my life. It was that initial visit that prompted me to begin my devotional nature blog, Words from the Wilderness. Estes Park became the inspiration for and epicenter of my contemporary fiction series, Climbing Higher. And most importantly, the mountains centered me—helped me navigate the still-unknown passages of my soul, calmed me in turbulent life seasons, provided a reassuring steadiness. In short, they became the home of my heart, and so much of what matters in my life is downstream of them.

But as transformative as the mountains have been for me, their Maker has been far more so.

You see, I believe in the God known as *El Shaddai* in Scripture—the God of the mountains. I believe in a faith that forges a way over even the most formidable of peaks. I believe in a kingdom more resplendent than a mountain sunrise. And I believe in a Love more patient than the peaks, more grounded than the granite, and more relentless than the rivers that pour out the melting snow. I believe, in part, because I have seen the mountains—and because I have seen them move.

So, my friend, that is my prayer for you. May grace fill your days like the aroma of the pine trees. May blessings sprinkle your path like alpine wildflowers. And may you hold the hand of that unconquerable Love on every step of your journey—onward and upward toward the High Country.

— Ashlyn McKayla Ohm
October 2024

ACKNOWLEDGMENTS

I have been blessed beyond measure to have never walked my trails alone. I'm forever grateful for the beautiful souls who not only help me on my own journey to the High Country, but also caught the sparks of my vision for *High Country Hymnal* and cheered this book, and its author, on.

For my friends and readers who pray for me, encourage me, and listen so lovingly to the stories I tell. I could fill a whole new book with your names, but know you are all so dear to me.

For my stellar cover designer, Hannah Linder. Thank you for patiently refining my vague ideas and creating a cover that captures the spirit of the book.

For my incredible parents, Ralph and Derri Ohm. You have always been the granite grace under my feet, the soaring sky over my head, and the sun that steadies me daily with made-new mercy. All that I am is because of your guiding hands and your unfailing hearts. I love you so much!

And for the God of the mountains—the Lord Who directs my days, the Author Who sings my story, the Love Who holds my heart. No words I could ever weave would capture the glory of all that You are! Thank You for being both the High Country to which I climb and the Son of Man Who walks the path with me. I trust You with all my trails both now and on the other side of the Great Divide. May these words be my worship, and may Your fire fall on these pages that I offer up to You.

PHOTO CREDITS

All photographs in this book were taken by my parents or me, except one. This exception is the mushroom photo on page 24, which was taken and graciously shared with me for this book by my dear friend Lena Johnson. The mushrooms pictured are Eastern American Jack-o'-lantern Mushrooms, scientifically known as *Omphalotus illudens*, and they are the bioluminescent fungi referred to in the preceding poem. I'm deeply grateful to Lena, not only for teaching me about wondrous glowing mushrooms, but also for carrying the light so faithfully herself.

ABOUT THE AUTHOR

A worshiper of the Creator and a wanderer of creation, Ashlyn McKayla Ohm is most at home where the streetlights die and the pavement ends. She finds her writer's calling at the intersection of honesty and hope, weaving stories, poems, and blog posts that offer light for any path. The author of the contemporary fiction Climbing Higher trilogy and the popular devotional *A Year in the Woods*, she has also seen her work published by Proverbs 31 Ministries, Awake Our Hearts, and Short Fiction Break. If she's not daydreaming about her next book, you'll find her hiking, birdwatching, or otherwise getting lost in the woods. Follow Ashlyn's writing at the links below!

Website: **ashlynmckaylaohm.com**

Instagram: **@wildernessashlyn**

Facebook: **Ashlyn McKayla Ohm, Author**

KEEP READING!

A Year in the Woods: 52 Weeks of Growth, Grace, and the Glory of God

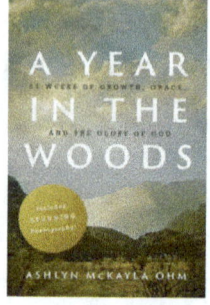

Step away from a stressful world and enjoy a full year of inspiration with this peaceful book—fifty-two nature-themed devotionals complete with full-color photography and space for journaling.

Climbing Higher Series: ***When the Ice Melts, Where the Wings Rise, Why the Moutains Stand***

Sisters Addisyn and Avery Miles have chosen different paths to cope with the fallout of their tumultuous past. But now, in the majesty of the Rocky Mountains, the two sisters must navigate threats from the past, new opportunities for the future, and the same fears that have always threatened to tear them apart, all while climbing higher...not only into the mountains but also toward the God Who still moves them.

Explore these books and more by visiting **ashlynmckaylaohm.com/my-writing** or scanning the code below!

PRAYERS, PRAISES, PROMISES

The following pages are a space for you to record your own thoughts about the mountains and the God Who still moves them. Go ahead and let your words wander.

HIGH COUNTRY HYMNAL

PRAYERS, PRAISES, PROMISES

HIGH COUNTRY HYMNAL

www.ingramcontent.com/pod-product-compliance
Lightning Source LLC
Chambersburg PA
CBHW050330010526
44119CB00004B/113